Small Poems
For Children

JOSH DOUGLAS

Edition JOSH DOUGLAS

Contents

Taste by Small Poem For Children.

The children are An inheritance des LORD . Solomon.

Preparing

See there some small poems prepared for the benefit of children. The creator know very well, that he, if poet, over there Through very few fame achieve can, but that used to be also are purpose not. He referred to bad only one useful truths Like this in rhyme recite that they were not beyond childish sensibility; and he has she Like this small made, on that she des at easier, Through single read, would be able to in It memory printed become, without that It necessary used to be, that they by outsidelearned became; something Where the maker very in return for is, and that in addition, single Through repeated read, occur can.

It no cause gave until It to formulate this one pieces is been - that the maker has children of his own, who are now his only and greatest pleasure - that one can such

pieces in our language lack has - that he also please for others useful is
- and that he the High German *Lieder für child* of WEISSE and the *little Lieder für little mädchen und junglinge* by G . W . BURMAN , of very a lot of pleasure, read has; also to have she it many times on Pine tree away assisted, beautiful he there actually none out translated, or taken over has.

They are all not suitable for children of four or five years, but this was also correct not necessary. Men can yourself to elect, which ones man On his children want to to leave read, also can man suddenly to notice, or An child understands what It is reading than not. The author has tested all of them, and he can assure that his eldest little boys - a child of five years - many of them, on the first or second reading, has understood; and therefore he maintains himself assured that all these bits for children, above the five and downstairs the ten years, usable are. Also allowed It no harm if here and there the childish mind has a little difficulty meet, and over there Through until to ask and to talk is becoming excited.

If I had the pleasure of having these words approved and with fruit were used, I would now and then, with pleasure, add a leaf to the none I currently On mine Countrymen offered. It number, that I currently grant, is bigenough, to there the trial co at to take.

At two dear little guys

... First for reward A kiss or two.

At two dear little guys

Look there, sweet wedges! A bundle of
bits, Entertained there you along!
And jumps to your dwelling, But... first ter
reward
A kiss or two.

Driven by loveHave I she sung,
And want ye there more,
Thou may there to to ask.
When she you please
Comes hopping weather.

It childlike luck.

I have toys, clothes-pen, milk and bread, A
cradle to in at to sleep.

It childlike luck

I am a child By God loved,
And until luck created.
   Are love is big;
I have toys, clothes-pen, milk and bread, A
   cradle to in at to sleep.

   I live feel free;
   I leather of lust;
I don't know of any worries yet. By it play
   tired,
I close my eyes at night, And sleep until On
   Pine tree tomorrow.

   Praised be God For it roomy enjoyment
Of so many favors! Mine heart and mouth
Will him every morning And each evening
   Prices.

The peach.

That peach my father gave me, To that I

industrious leather.

The peach

That peach my father gave me, To that I
industrious leather.
Now I eat satisfied and happy. That peach
tastes Unpleasant more.

The cheerfulness belongs to the youth That
Educational zig shows.
The industriousness, that childish virtue, Is
becoming always well rewarded.

The childhood love.

And I go hopping by his side', Also than

entertained and learns he me;

The childhood love

Mine father is mine Best friend.
   He calls me still are dear child. k Save it,
without anxious at fear.
And I go hopping by his side', Also than
entertained and learns he me;
There can no better father being!

I'm also sometimes naughty, But if mine
vice me repents,
Then his father's heart is moved, Then his
love speaks no reproach, Yes even, when
he me chastises,
Than see I tears in are eyes.

Should I by disobedience, Than to make,
that mine father cries;
Would I make him sigh and complain; Nay,
if my youngness do wrong,Than fall I soon
it at foot,
And shall On God forgiveness to ask.

Alexis.

But if she on, that it pleases, For her, to

play with, asks, Than is becoming That
love race reduced;

Alexis

Alexis loves his sisters, When she in peace
to live;
He calls her yourself are sweetheart,
If she will give him her toys. But if she on,
that it pleases, For her, to play with, asks,
Than is becoming That love race reduced;
And if she prevents him from doing his
will, Than hate he almost her whole.
Also is she through it at a lot of,
When she above it Through someone is
becoming praised.

* * *

A love, That Like this race cools,
Who wickedly aims at his own advantage,
Would that well straight love being?

The true wealth.

What is wealth anyway? what is honor?
God friend at being is a lot of more;

The true wealth

Let no money delight our young minds, But
holiness and virtue.
Wisdom is the most necessary good; It
jewelry by the youth.

What is wealth anyway? what is honor? A
handful void mud.
To be God's friend is much more; That Jesus
love, is rich.

Come we fall at our God's feet, To virtue and
holiness:
This is how our young mind becomes on
earthTen heaven prepared.

Then we'll get that dear darling, That never
again perishes.
Then we walk on the path of virtue, And to
startle for It angry.

It cheerful learn.

Mine hoop, mine prick toll exchange I for books;

It cheerful learn

My playing is learning, my learning is playing, And Why would me than It learn bored?

Reading and writing amuses me. I exchange my hoop, my pricking top for books; I want to in mine prints mine pastime to search,
it Is wisdom, it are virtues, Unpleasant which ones I hook.

It pity.

Who that I ever see wearing sorrow, k
Have also feeling over there by.

It pity

Who that I ever see wearing sorrow, k Have
  also feeling over there by.
I do not close my ear to his lamentation, But
  Help it if I can.

To lift a man in sorrow, Is even for kids
  sweet.
Who can mock with those who mourn,
  Shows An bad mind.

Would I otherwise rejoice? Would k
  laughing in are smart?
Oh no, a noble pity Suits On mine children's
  heart.

I will then lament with sorrowful ones,
  Them to console in their pain.
To help bear another's burden, Shall mine
  pleasure are.

The industriousness.

Mine classes want to I learn,

The industriousness

to sleep long in the morning, At yawn and
at to yawn,
   Sat ugly for An child. Who always has to
understand a lot, And crazy language want
to clap,
Sees seldom zig loved.

Would I spend my time At thousand
trifles?
   I don't take advantage of that. Mine
classes want to I learn,
Mine masters shall I honor,
Than become I hast An man.

The mirror.

Want to k know, Who I am,
Then God's word must be the mirror,
Where I mine heart out know.

The mirror

Who always looks in the mirror, And zig of
   beauty flatters;
Don't realize the true beauty, But hunts
   Unpleasant vanity.

This glass makes us proud, or gives us pain;
   Want to k know, Who I am,
Then God's word must be the mirror, Where
   I mine heart out know.

complains by Pine tree little ones William.

Ah! mine sisters is died

complains by Pine tree little ones William on the dead by are sisters

Ah! mine sisters is died,
    only fourteen months old. k Saw her
dead in it box lie:
    oh well what used to be mine little
sister cold! k Called out her add: mine
dear Sissy!
    Sissy! Sissy! but for not.Ah! her eyes are
Closed;
    I must cry with sorrow.Always want to I
to her mourn,
    scattering flowers on her grave:
weeping On the kisses think,
That me it dear girl gave.
Tomorrow I will - but for me toois it danger
    by die big.
Yesterday she played with me; yesterday
    yet! and now - already dead!

It gift.

k Have you tog Like this sweet if he

It gift

Mother dear! see a rose thereBy your Coosjen,
    while ye today birthday are.
I sang this morningAnd jumped:
    Like this desired I Unpleasant serve time.

But can't I dig rhymes,Must I shut up
    For mine brother in poetry.
Then take it, mother! bad this roses By your
    Coosjen,
    k Have you tog Like this sweet if he.

Little Claar.

Welcome dear little sister!
Welcome in this to live!

Welcome greeting by Little Claar for her little little sister

Welcome dear little sister!
    Welcome in this to live!
baker! can't i have a kissAt mine little sister
    to give.

    Do you want to sleep? O she chalk!
        It will surely bore her. Tomorrow, if ye
    awake are,
    Shall I of you play.

Rest easy, then thou shalt grow up; Learn
    tog soon walk!
When you sit on mother's lap, Shall she toys
    buy.

O! Mamatjen is Like this Good!
    Everything want to she to give,
If only her children sweet And at peace to
    live.

The idleness.

Pray, learn, write, read, To play, to work
has are time.

The idleness

Never must I be empty; Everything doing of
lust and diligence.
Pray, learn, write, read, To play, to work has
are time.

Mother dear can't take it much either, That
the time neglected is becoming.
To be lazy, she says, is to steal time, And us
to live is Like this short!

It doggies.

_ can An beast Like this satisfying areWhat wait man not by me!

It doggies

How grateful is my little dogFor little bones
and what bread!
He wags his tail, he walks around, And
jumps on mines shot.

Meat and bread and wine are given me,And
often delicacy:
But can a beast be so grateful, What wait
man not by me!

It broken glass.

come Keesje sweet! love on of chalk,

The broken glass One narration

Cornelis had broken a glassFor On the street.

Though he had deprived the pieces,He knew no council.

He was afraid to lie,while God It sees:

And would he cheat on Mama now, That could he not.

He stood dismayed and moved, The mother comes:

She sees the tears in his eyes, He shone dumbfounded.

Has Keesje, she said, what skilled?

What saves there On?

'I love,' he said, mother! in a moment Weather angry done.

While working on palettes Bee it window used to be.

Flew my *volan* , through the hefty rockets,Over there in It glass.

But if your Keesje it of his lifeNot again do,

Then you want to forgive him,Thou are Like this Good!

Come on dear! stop chalking,Said mother when:

I don't want to blame you for that mistake, He got An kiss.

Who always wants to speak the truth, Is
   becoming well rewarded.
Who seeks lies for his flaws, Is becoming never
   changed.'

The religiosity.

How Nice stands me this wreaths!

The religiosity

If in the dear spring
The flowers decorate the field, Then I pick
rose buds, Violets, virgin sweethearts,
lemon herb and lilacs.
Then I will weave wreaths, And wear That
ter honor
By God, That me It to live
And donated flowers. Than sing I: King of
Heaven!
You make violets grow, With roses,
maidens, lemon herb and lilacs,
With a thousand thousand flowers; To
yours power and love
At children at show.
How beautiful these wreaths look on me!
Ah leave me not forget
That ye It have doing to grow!

The hare.

Look Pietje! look, An hare,

The hare

Look Pietje! look! An hare, O That Like this soon could walk!

No, said the smart Pete, Want ye An bunnies are, I not:
k Want to rather slowly to go, than it of Pine tree dead buy.

* * *

He who is always to be praised Of abilities That he has

Live contentedly and gratefully, Can are gifts well spend.

But that he who always kneels And what andren are want to being,

Even what he has loses, Have I more than at sometime read.

Narration by Dorisje.

We drunk chocolate, And did hundred to ask.

One narration by Dorisje

We were recently with *Saartje* , Our old
good baker, Who can tell fairy tales. We
drunk chocolate,
And did hundred to ask.

In the end our *Saartje said* :Well now, my
sweethearts! Thou knows the four tides,
What holds ye for It Best?

Then my sister *Mietje said* , That time is
my dearest, When the trees Bloom.
Then you get beautiful flowers, To
bunches by at flattened.
Then one sees a thousand birds On green
twigs to sing.
Is that not in the spring?

Winter, dear *Saartje* ! Said *Pietjen* , is the
best, Then we hear,And drinks chocolate,
Or eat thick waffles.

No, I prefer summer *Keesje* said , then it's
fair.Than hoof I not at learn.

But I said, it is It Best
If most the fruits ripe are.

Then it is good to snap. Then you have apricots, And plums, and morello cherries,
And peaches and pears:
And is that not in it autumn?

Listen, children, said *Saartje*, The winter must the fields And gardens fertile to make.
One must prune the trees; The field must be fattened; That do man in Pine tree winter.
The trees must bloom, To give us fruits; That doing she in the spring.
The fruits must grow; They do that in the summer. One must reap the fruits; That do man in it autumn.

So must you, dear children! In all seasons Praise God's wise goodness, And well at peace being.

Jesus.
An Vocal part.

Jesus is An children's friend!

Jesus
A song piece Little Claar and Johnny

at together.
Jesus is a child's friend! Ours want to he zig have mercy. He took children in his arms:Jesus is An children's friend!

CLAART ONLY .
Oh, were Jesus still on earth! Soon flew I Unpleasant it to.

JANTJE only.
Ah used to be Jesus yet on soil!
k Flew of you Unpleasant Jesus to.

at together.
Son of God! who lives forever!Hear us beg, And forgives
Our boldness and flaws! Son of God! who lives forever! Bless our youth, and give, That We often by YOU speak!

The floating top.

Never runs mine floating top without to
succeed;

The floating top

My floating top never runs without blows;
   Because love I on, than runs he not. I have
   in already that to beat sadness,
And shall to other toys to ask.

    But isn't it the same with Flipje? Yes; I
never had to fear blows, k Would seldom
in mine books read,
And that gives father also sadness.

Shame I have to learn from a spinning top,
   To work diligently without coercion. k
   Want to, until mine punishment, mine for
life
No other toys to go desire.

The plum tree.

Johnny got are hat full plums,

The plum treeOne narration

Jantje once saw plums hanging, O! if Eggs
Like this big.

It seemed that Jantje wanted to go pick,
beautiful are father it it forbade.

Here is, he said, nor my father, nor the
gardener, who sees it: At An tree, Like this
full loaded,

one does not miss five six plums. But I
want to obedient being,

and not pick: I walk to. Would I, for a
handful of prunes,disobedient being? No.

Forth went Jantje: but his father, That it
quiet listened to had,

Met him while walking in front of the
middle path. Come my little Johnny, said
the father, come mine little sweetheart!

Now I will pick you plums; now has father
Johnny sweet.

Then Papa started shaking, Johnny picked
up suddenly on;

Johnny got his hat full of plums,and walked
to on An gallop.

The beggar.

Who looks upon him with admiration, Do
Unpleasant it command by Jesus not.

The beggar

That decrepit man, who sits almost naked,
And trembling with cold, begging me for a
dime, Is for a bit Good if I. God wisdom
gave only
Me what more money than it. Ben I than
better?... No.
A pious and honest man often wears dirty
clothes, I want to than also the virtue in
poor people honor.
Who looks upon him with admiration, Do
Unpleasant it command by Jesus not.

The true friendship.

That seldom praises, speaks friend language.

The true friendship

A friend, who shows me my faults,
Severely punished, and never excused,
Has on my heart a great power: But the
low heart that always flatters, Suspect I
by selfishness,
I can are presence not tolerate.
Who seldom praises, speaks friendly
language. That always flatters, lies many
times.

It seed shall it serve.

David

Preparing

I am much too sensitive about the favorable reception which my *little poems give have had children* with my compatriots, than that my joy and gratitude, because of this, not openly express would. The oral and written declarations of the pleasure caused by these my humble labors, to have me often strong affected; Yes often called out I bee such occasions out:

Tears flow from my eyes , Dear children, if you me asks to more poetry.

Ah! my heart, so moved, Bless God, who liveth forever , That he me That joy gives!

It is therefore no slowness, no lethargy been, That me It advance of this labor has shifted for so long. What then? - sheer inability, my dear compatriots! As a poet especially, I cannot work when I want to; and as soon as I have to force myself, everything turns out badly. I waited then, until that I again in That condition hit, in which I mine firsts manufactured have; and it is the fruit of those hours, which I now offer again to our children; in heap that the same for a bit Like this to be allowed to please if the firsts.

I had long mine thoughts to leave to go, and even only one resources employed, to some art pictures with these nursery rhymes too add, when Mr. ALLART , *Bookseller at Amsterdam* , one and away pointed out, to over there in until mine pleasure to pass. The pictures will pass under my supervision Painter J. _ BUYS signed, and by the Heeren PUNT and VAN DER MORE be engraved; by the skill of which may be seen in the fine pictures for Gellerts fables; which pictures one, Like this well if That fables, On our Dutch youth not enough can recommend.

These pictures will be set as low as possible, and the rhymes, however are available separately. They, however, who zig from the first and best prints provided want, pleasen, bee theirs booksellers,

or bee JOSH DOUGLAS , at *Amsterdam* , or bee the WED . J . V . JOSH DOUGLAS *here* , theirs specify names; will make the first prints to such as soon as possible, become Delivered.

Goodbye mine Compatriots! and be insured, that It me always An sensitive it will be a pleasure to be able to do something for the use or amusement of you or your children inflict.

* * *

I must add here that there are reasons which compel me, for none copies for egt at acknowledge, than That Through the printers this one single handedly Sosigned are.

the Wed J by JOSH DOUGLAS

Lottie and Keesje.

What good is it that you are lonely in An
nook sit, and complains.

Lottie and Keesje

KEESJE
Say me sweet dear *Lottie* !
   what is the cause, that you cry: Hebtge
your bracket bag lost,
or broken, dear girl?

LOT
Wouldn't I cry, dear *Keesje* ! mother sweet
   used to be not met
With my sewing oh! she saw me of sadness
   and sadness On.
Yes she wild me not to kiss, Like this if she
   otherwise always do.
Fie me! ah! that such a mother to mine
   naughtiness mourn must.

KEESJE
What good is it that you are lonely in An
   nook sit, and complains.
   go, she shall It you to forgive,
   if ye to change asks.

LOT
Will you then intercede for me, me guide:

KEESJE
Yes sure:

Wouldn't I speak for *Lottie* , That mine Dear
  sisters is.
But you need no intercession, if ye mother
  fall at foot,
Will she surely forgive you, Mother, know
  thou, is Like this Good.
    Yeastren read she for us both,
        that also God forgives the guilt: k Know,
    she shall you clear change,
    over there she such An example has.

The health.

Who never has enough for his mouth,
Lives seldom cheerful and healthy.

The health

Health is a great treasure To pleased at to
  live.
Though I had great wealth, What benefit
  would It to give,
  So I, gnawed with fear and pain, Me selves
  until An burden had to are.

But would I take my Father's advice Not
  diligent involve?
And gluttony and excess Not avoid and
  forgot?
  Who never has enough for his mouth,
  Lives seldom cheerful and healthy.

Little boy and Keetje.

Learn now first, than to play We.

Little boy and Keetje

CLEAR

Always working, always reading, That
must well sad being:
   Is that why one lives? Funny Keetje!
playing now;Ah! the time must you bored
Serve ye On your masters gives.

KEET

Never to work, never to read, Always in
Pine tree garden at being,
   Is that why one lives? Little girl dear,
stop playing;Ah! the time must you bored,
Serve ye On your dolls gives.

CLEAR

Sometimes playing, sometimes reading,
That shall well It Best being,
Keetje sweet! come play of me.

KEET

It will surely bore you. On at to hold by It
to play:
Learn now first, than to play We.

* * *

Ter more closely need had Keetje this

said,
Or Little boy had, ashamed, her dolls
reserved.

It found it songs.

Which An sweet and nice songs!

It found it songs

I just found this piece of paperk Heap that I
   It read can.
Above it is written:How! ...

THE PLEASED MAN

Come, children, sit down with me.k Shall you
   An songs to give.
The contentment is much more Than to
   estimate in this to live.

Though I have little, I have enough; Would I
   An man envy Pine tree,
Who always wore beautiful clothes, But heavy
   pain had to suffering.

Working always keeps me healthy And quick
   by body and members.
I wake up in the morning Refreshed and well
   at peace.

The hunger that I said miss, Do me a lot of
   more eager eat,
Than if I at a king's table, Used to be day On
   day seated.

I often have water out a source Of more taste
   drunk,

Than ever the wine could give me, Bee cups
poured in.

And the day has passed, See I Pine tree
evening rise,
Then I'll put on a songTo mines God at Prices.

Now dear children, live like me, Rejoices you
in God blessing!
Say thanks every moment, What have I a lot of
got!

* * *

What sweet and sweet songs! How pleases
and hits It me.
May I learn to live like this, Satisfied man! if
ye.

The good   ambition.

I can It not forget,
But it shall not weather to happen.

The good   ambition One complains by Daantje

Ah me! I am sad, I lost the prize Serve father sweet promised had,
To him who learned best. That book with beautiful pictures, Of green silk ribbons, What I longed for Has Johnny now got;
Because he could write best, And it fastest used to be in It read.
Yes on the cards he could The lands and rivers, The seas and the towns,
It fastest by all find.

But would I envy him, And now yet fewer learn?
Nay, I will praise his gifts, And it at more love.
But also I will delay, Pine tree honorary prize at to win,
Which Father has promised again. k Want to than what fewer to play, I want to what shorter to sleep,
And taller diligence spend
In hearing the lessons, Which my masters give me. By playing too much By sleeping too long, By looking around, When I had to pay attention Have I Pine tree price lost.

That book with beautiful pictures, With
green silk ribbons Has Johnny that got!
I can It not forget,
But it shall not weather to happen.

The watchman.

Would I for Pine tree clapper fear,

The watchman

Should I fear the clapper, O! That dear brave
   man
Makes me rest easy And also safe to sleep
   can.
   Mother dear! I firmly believe That he on
   the thieves suits.

Clean he walks through wind and rain, it To
   sing is becoming he never tired:
Good God! give him your blessing, But my
   eyes are closing. Dear clapper! love the
   wait
   I go to sleep: good night!

Klaasje and Pietje.

Leave it come, if he can.

Klaasje and Pietje

CLASS
Pietje, if you don't want to be good, Than appears the black man.

PETE
Klaasje, that's a lie! Let him come if he can. Who believes in such a man, Is by are mind robbed.

Winter song.

Ah! how many a thousand people to have
Like this a lot of stock not.

Winter song

I see the yellow leaves fall, of Pine tree
　　summer is it done:
And the howling of snow and rain
　　announces us Pine tree winter On.
　　Ah! how vibrate me the members,
　　k Walk Unpleasant it nooks by Pine tree
　　fireplace;
Father say: in such An cold serves there
　　wood nor peat spared.
o We have so much stockfor Pine tree skimp
　　winter time;
There they put me in warm clothes for Pine
　　tree strands frost frees.
Winter pears, cabbage, and apples butter,
　　meat, Yes what not already,
Already in our basement, that us Tasty
　　flavours shall.
May I be thankful now, about mine happy
　　lot;
Yes I want to live obedientlyand you thank,
　　good God!
Yes I want to think all the time if the cold
　　me sadness,
Ah! how many a thousand people to have
　　Like this a lot of stock not.
Yes, I want to save some money and what
　　by mine abundance

At An poor baby to give,
that by hungry cry must.

God goodness.

God is good, that's where the rain falls On
It dehydrated country:

God goodness

God is good, that's where the rain falls On
the parched land: Father bath to such An
blessing,
Without rain,
Say he, grows no herb nor plant.

Dear drops, fall to the earth! Fall in great
ones abundance,
Gold is not of such value For our soil.
God interrogates us: God is Good!

God wisdom.

God is wise, that gentle rainHolds now on:

God wisdom

God is wise, that gentle rainHolds now on: It
  arid grass
Got so much vogt again, If for it to grow
  necessary used to be.

  Fell there already at heavy rain,
    Never saw sunshine, Than would it
  longer not until blessing,
  But until injury for us are.

God is wise, that gentle rain Holds weather
  on: the arid ground
Got so much vogt now, If God wisdom
  necessary found.

The generous retaliation.

k Shall her by mine goodies to give,

The generous retaliation

Would I torment my sister? To that she me
  not loves?
Would I speak ill of her? No I think: she is An
  child!

I'll give her some of my goodies Than what
  grapes, than An pear,
Then a hazelnut six seven, And when she
  want to, yet more.

I will win her heart with love, She is tog no
  malignant child;
Like this long shall I her love, Until she in it
  end me also loves.

It sick child.

Mine heads! ah! It do Like this very!

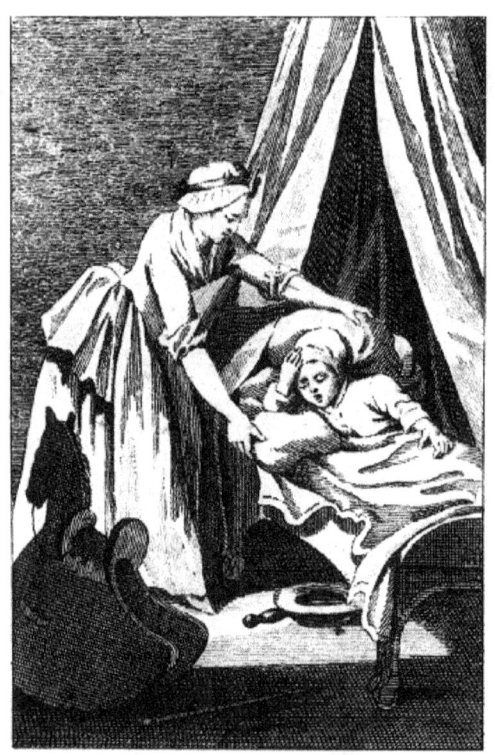

It sick child

My heads! ah! it hurts so much! It appears
   by An cloven;
   No rocking horse amuses me anymore;
   And beautiful man asks, what I desire
   I disgust by it tastiest eat.

Though no child lies as low as I, The peace is
   me taken.
   And sleep I at sometime An moment,
   Than become I awake of An fright
   By means of it nasty dream.

Now I first become, by what I lack, Until
   gratitude driven:
   Now I feel, but with sadness, How much
   one owes to God, If man healthy allowed
   to live.

   But oh! that God is always good; I want to
   now satisfying being,
   And though I must suffer pains, Patient
   say: God is Good!
   He can me weather cured.

It good   example.

Come, my darlings, let us live until each
other utility and joy!

It good   example

Father lives with our motheralways pleased
  and pleased,
O how they love each other, never grunt she
  if We.

Shows one something to desire, than say
  the other: that is Good!
Mother is the best if she something for
  father do.

Father attempts always at know
    what is mother's wish; And It no her
  may bored,
  gives On father sadness.

Father gave the Best peach
    last to mother with a kiss; He wish
  yourself there not by eat:
  little boy, would We this doing?

Dearest sister, dearest brothers O It
  stretches us until reproach, That We often
  Like this squabble;
  oh well ye know not how it me sorry.

Come, my darlings, let us live until each
  other utility and joy!

Let us try to follow fathers love and
mothers virtue.

There alone can love dwell, over there only
is it to live sweet,
Where one, happy and unconstrained, for
each other everything do.

Pietje and Keetje.

PIET .
Well: I have four nice prints,
KETTLE .
I two ribbons,
Good for her, directly I guess.

Pietje and Keetje

PETE

Come my dear sweet sister,Give me An kiss,
   O I am Like this in mine arrange!
     I have heard from mother, That *Camie*
by it school shall come,
No one is Like this pleased if I.

KEET

Then let's think of something,To at donate
   At That dearest girl.
   If we just tell her something.And no deeds
that accompany
Is it no straight cheerfulness.

PETE

Well: I have four nice prints,

KEET

I two ribbons,
Good for her, directly I guess.

PETE

It will please her, however small, Since
then she need not ask, Or it bee us but
talk is.

It patience.

This saw I last in our cat,

It patience

Patience is such a virtue To in An difficult task

    Are eye white to be carried out; I saw this in our cat the other day, That hours long dived fed up,

To on An rat at lurk.

She did not go till she the rat, Captured, in her claws had.

A religious youth.

Whom God loves That is becoming are child;

A religious youth makes An lucky ones old age

The one in his youth It path der virtue
has smashed, And do goodWait good cheer
his old to dawn.

But those are timeUseless wears out,
His fresh powers of sin gives, Must,
decrepit, Sadness expect.

Leave than, O youth!
It path der virtue,
You asked please, Then you will be happy
By remorse free
Yours old to dawn.

Though you are a mockery By their, That
God
too naughty forsaken, You have much more
Than money or honor
By it at wait.

Whom God loves That is becoming are
child;
And must he die, She asked or spae,He shall
grace
Bee God acquire.

The coal tit.

Now say I bee me yourself: there are no
birds more.

The coal tit

My snap had only been hanging in the tree
for an hour,Or this coal tit fed up there in.
Then I said to myself: How shall I catch
birds!That is called first right An Good get
started!

But ah! It are well seven to dawn,
I saw not a chaffinch or a great tit in all
that time,Now am I all ter down beaten,
Now say I bee me yourself: there are no
birds more.

.

That already at great stuff wait,
To that it in it get started are attempts
succeed,
Is as foolish as it is driven to despair, To
that he for An time for adversity must
stoop.

Pietje bee It sickbed by are sisters.

'Good Jesus! hear my lamentation, 'And recovery mine little sister weather.

Pietje bee It sickbed by are sisters

Oh that moaning, oh that complaining, Can mine tender heart not wear,
Sissy dear I feel your pain! k Would willing for you suffering,
Could it free you from sorrow, Or but until relief are.

But it is beyond my means; But I bend, of weeping eyes,
Praying my knees down. 'Don't let my prayer displease you Good Jesus! hear my lamentation, And recovery mine little sister weather.

Don't let her live, Ah mine mother would it die,
Father certainly went to the grave. Dear God! where was Pete? Namet ye of mine little sister Sissy
Also mine parents by me off.'

It interrogated prayer.

What will my grateful heart serve good ones God retaliate?

It interrogated prayer

My sisters is healthy. God heard my prayer! And has until our joy mine little sister sweet rescued.

What shall my grateful heart render to the good God? Like this big An God want to That thanks are by An child?

Yes! Father says God is pleased with that, Dies shall I his praise, already am I young, to report.

It tenderhearted child.

Good God! oh let her live Until mine
benefit until mine joy,

It tenderhearted child

Wouldn't I honor my mother, Ah what
doeze not for me ?
What is my use I may learn; Ben I cheerful,
she is pleased.

Am I sick, I hear her complain; And when
she bee me sit
With an eye lifted high, Than believe I, that
she prays.

Yes than prays she, that I soon Allowed
liberated are by mine smart:
If I get better, how cheerfully And how
satisfying is her heart.

I will always love her, Always doing, that
her pleases.
I never want to start anything Over there
mine mother about complains.

I will call her name with reverence, If she
descends in It grave.
And praise God's goodness forever, That me
such An mother gave.

Good God! oh well leave her to live
To my advantage, to my delight, What a

sadness it would give me,Her at to miss in mine youth.

The carelessness.

A o'clock by carelessness Can to make that man weeks cries.

The carelessness

See Keesje! this dead mosquito Flew so
happily and swiftly, But it is through
indifference, That he now dead on table
slate.

He had such a sense in the candlelight,
And flew there careless in.
Now is he over there; but it is at leave;
There is no advice for the mosquito now.
He was deceived by appearances. O! leave
us this until apprentice are,
That, before doing anything important,
One has to think for a long time. A o'clock
by carelessness Can to make that man
weeks cries.

The bird on the stool.

Mine bird, ah! condemns me.

The bird on the stool

It are pass six or seven to dawn,
That I this cisje cog by Klaas Pine tree bird
man;
And though at first I had to lament my
trouble, Now is there nowhere no, That
better to fly can.

How would I progress If I Like this
Educational used to be if he!
But I would almost cry. Mine bird, ah!
condemns me.

I want to behave like this before then,
That, honor I me until play arrange,
I can ask myself without fear: Who learns
there better, he or I?

**Second continuation of the Kleine
gedigten children, by mr. JOSH
DOUGLAS .**

At mine little readers.

Possible is it the last bundle;

At mine little readers

Don't say, my dear wedges, That . you
    forgets;
I have something to give youOnly one hours
    weather spent.
It may be the last bundle; Belongs! ye have
    there also enough.
    it Is in it number not convenient;
    And for bigger is it what early.

Read little, well, and oftenLearns It best, in
    yours time:
Larger books you will get, If ye also what
    bigger are.

Johnny and It rabbit.

I have at few to that dear animal at buy;

Johnny and It rabbit

Over there see I An rabbit!
What would k happy are,
If I had it to walk in our garden, Said Jan:
but beautiful k mine money
Already thrice have counted,
I have too little to buy that sweet animal;
And beautiful me this On it heartily go,
I know no council! ...

* * *

Well! then let yourself learn this case,
Mine dear Jan!
That a wise child should not covet things,
That he at forward know, that he not to
get can.

The singing William.

God, he cried, is so good, That I it praise must!

The Singing William morning song

When going up the sun Was William
sitting at a well, Of good heart, to sing; He
had last nightInvigorating spent;
And couldn't contain it any longer. God,
called out he, is Like this Good,
That I it praise must!

Mighty Creator! I owe you, That I awoke
healthy and delighted.
Wise Ruler! I owe Jesus That I you know in
It first by mine youth.

Praise you the morning, I will also honor
you, That ye me advantageous in it to live
keeps;
Praise the morning, oh may it teach me, Holy
and satisfying at to live on earth.

To be diligent, obedient, and merry, Is me
until benefit and it is your commandment.
Kind Creator! who would not fear you! Who
you not honor, almighty God!

From you alone I must expect everything;
Who is if ye all-enough and mild.
To-day I will observe your laws; Over there
ye also children to bless want.

The little singer.

She horse smiling voice and strings;

The little singerEvening song
The light of the sunBegan
Alreê at languish;
The Moon
Ving On
To shine as clean as ever;When dear Cris,
A girl, I guess Of eight or nine years, Her
little zither took,
And hopping bee me came;
She laughingly combined voice and
strings;And sang It cheerful evening song,
That ye here Unsubscribed sees.

May the sun shine on herIn it West doing
valleys,
   This doesn't make me smart. God also
created Pine tree night to at to sleep,
Dies praises It mine heart.

How dark it may bek need not at fear
   In the dead of night.God will take care of
me Until that me the tomorrow
Weather cheerful expects.

No sorrow shall me naked;
God want to me to guard,

Already am I An child.
God shows, through me, lifeAnd food at to

give,
How He me loves.

The starry twinkling Cheered up It dark;
  The shining moon Begins on the
pasture Her shine at to spread,
And plays Through the blow.

Even if you don't see colors, Men is
becoming tog Through smells
  Refreshed wherever one goes. I even
hear in lilacs Pine tree nightingale to sing,
And it quail hit.

may i raise you up, Than close I mine eyes
  Don't worry, O mine God!
  YOU honor at to give,
And thankful to live,Is it blissful lot.

The wrong fear.

One need not be afraid, If man intends
angry at doing.

The wrong fear

Keesje saw at sometime Jews walk, To *what old! what old!* at buy;
He grew frightened, yes, pale with fright; He crawled away and started crying. Pietje mocked of that take shelter; And said laughing: do if I!

Kees said: wouldn't you be alarmed, If ye their at sometime On saws to call?
No, I can, Pietje then said: Why would I always fear? Men needs bad anxious at orphans,
If man intends angry at doing.

The love until It native country.

And, become I at sometime An man,
Like this useful are for it country, if I but
being can

The love until It native country

Already am I but An child,
Yet my Fatherland is most loved by me; I
became there in born;
I have there drink and food;
I allowed there it education
Hear from wise masters. I have parents,
friends in it, whom I love with all my
heart; I can there safe live;
That's why I will show myself grateful;
And, become I at sometime An man,
Like this useful are for it country, if I but
being can.

The vegging guys.

Ha! no folly is so great, Than at sweep without need.

The vegging guys

GIJSJE
Let us settle this quarrel, By means of at sometime brave together at sweep!

CLASS
I don't want; I have no desire to beat; But leave us Unpleasant Father to go;
I don't want to offend you; Father allowed It verdict to smoothe.

GIJSJE
Cowardly boy, without courage!

CLASS
O! think first what do.

GIJSJE
k Barrel you soon bee the dress:

CLASS
Wait, I'd defend myself then; k Ben Like this min afraid if ye.

GIJSJE
Is that Where, come than ter she!

CLASS

Nay: I will watch for that; But your to threaten *here* forgot.
Ha! no folly is so great, Than at sweep without need.

Here became she disturbed.
Daddy sweet had It correct heard.
He who was a warrior, and often in his life Of his policy and courage had given many trials, Said it's the best hero; he has the greatest courage; That brave sweep can, but it never unnecessary do.

It storm.

How beautiful shoot over there the lightning down!

It storm

How beautifully the lightning strikes there!
How stately rolls the Thunder!
The clouds gather, or drift to and fro;
While I in that already, formidable
Heavenly Lord!
Your Majesty admire.

Now is it past: An fresh air
Surround me wherever I go, and make the
birds sing. I see An new ones shine on
tree and field and fruit;
But, eternal God! you keep going, Even in
your blessings.

* * *
  *

What do I see, Cat! how, you tremble? Ah
want over there never for fear!
it Is An gift, that God us gives,
And therefore, dear girl, had to Caatje
satisfying being.

Little Claar bee the painting by hers deceased mother.

That sweet and smiling being,

Little Claar bee the painting by hers deceased mother

When I sat down Calmly contemplate the imageBy mine dear mother,
Then my tears roll Steady down the cheeks. That sweet and smiling creature,
Where godliness and sincerity gracefulness and joy Like this finished on is at read,
Then make me weep bitterly, Because I have to miss her;I - yet no nine years.
What have I not had for hours Sitting with her with benefit, When they play me,It An and other learned.
But I'll always remember,How she me bee her die
For it last yet at sometime embraced.

I can't think about it And k do It tog Like this please.

When she said: 'dear Little Claar! Your mother will soon die, And separate from this earth, To in the rejoice Heaven
Bee the angels at live; Then hear my last words,And give me it last kiss.

Honor God, love your father! Grow up in
virtue and wisdom! And wilt cheerful to
live,
Learn early the sins hate.
But have you ever done evil, Than must it
generous confess;
And God to Jesus will Shall you
forgiveness donate.
But look, my little Claar! On soil me not
again,
See often Unpleasant Pine tree heaven,
And say - that's where my mother lives.
ah, saw I after your die
My child also appear there, How would I
me rejoice.
And thank God reverently. For you, my
dear Claartje! Is also the heaven Open.

But oh well; my sweet girl! I feel death
approaching And can not longer speak.
Farewell, farewell, Claartje! Over there
have it last kiss!'

I went down crying; And it lasted few
hours,
Or mother used to be died.

When I now, seated
By the image of my mother, remembering

her death, Than roll me steady
The tears running down the cheeks. Than
see I Unpleasant Pine tree heaven,
My mother's home; Than call I, bitter
crying, O God, have ye That mother At me
Like this early deprived,
I must not rebuke you, How very I her
regretted;
Nay, thou art wise and holy, may I love
you, Mine dear Father honor, And take
mother's lessons, Then I will die with me
Bee YOU and mother come.
What shall that blissful being!

The withered rose.

The Creator, whom it behooves us to fear,
Is becoming Through bed never praised.

The withered rose

Why does the rose wither so quickly?Said
Jantjen: oh or it otherwise used to be!
God was also, methinks, more praised,Zoo
it rose longer Remained in being.

* * *
*

Though you think you see through it,Mine
dear Jan! It is Like this not.
The Creator knows best of all,Why it must
fall off so quickly; And want to also, dat
watches,
How race It terrestrial beautiful perishes.
The Creator, whom it behooves us to fear,
Is becoming Through bed never praised.

Sissy bee It harpsichord.

If only I could learnI did mine best if ye.

Sissy bee It harpsichord

Those lovely tones Please me alree;
  Already have I few years,
  I would love to sing along. When my
oldest brothersOn it harpsichord plays,
Then he asks me, mockingly, Or not me
not race bored?
Than say I, dear boy!
  o Please play long for me! May I It also
but learn,
  I did my best like you. The day before
yesterday used to be I birthday,
  And mother then asked me, What I by
her coveted;
  I gave her a kiss first, And said: mine
sweet mommy!
  Do me this favor, That I allowed learn
play,
  And sing to the arts. She took me in her
arms,
  And said: in the new year. Now fire I by
desire,
Ah came the master but.

* * *

The youth is eager to playAnd to sing useful
  out,
And is one tired of learning, Than gives this

sweet sound
Again new lust and strength; Like this lives
man pleased and sweet;
And joyfully shuns company, That often
wander do.

It wise answer.

He has On us are law out love only datum,

It wise answer

You ask me why I am obedient to God;it Is
therefore, that I It if show and Good
acknowledge.
He has given us his law out of love alone,
On that We pleased and cheerful would to
live;
And already what us That law prohibits,
Is, however it may seem, not to our
advantage, Want to someone than happy
being,
That leather obedient God at fear.

It known.

I never have more pleasure than when I do my dutyCheerful have performs.

It known

I never have more pleasure than when I do
    my dutyCheerful have performs.
Then the food tastes best; then I can jump
    merrily;And happy songs to sing;
But if I am slow or naughty, I am not at
    ease;Than have I none lust
In food, drink, or play; then I become aware
    permanently blamed,
That I'm a slutcake, and that I'll never be a
    man,Zoo doing, become can.

A letter by Carl On are little sister Caatje.

Therefore talk I on it paper.

A letter by Carl On are little sister Caatje

Sister dear! I will let you know, That I, since
   your departure,
been sitting in my room Girl sweet! of An
   stiff neck.
Hello, I'll write to you sometime, Because It
   again is Like this bleak,
That I always have to stay at home, And that
   tastes not on Pine tree duration.
I have quite something to talk to you; Often
   think I, was she here!
But that thinking is of no avail, Therefore
   talk I on it paper.
One must write, Papaatje says, For a bit Like
   this, if or man talk;
Therefore I will, dear Caatje, YOU narrate,
   how it me go.
I was grumpy at first, that Clorinde YOU by
   house and of zig took;
I was glad that she loved you, But what
   doeze at Amsterdam,
   Said I - was she here remained;
   I would like her to be my best picture
   For An new Year datum;
   Oh we are so used to together. But what
   helped tog already that complain,
   Cat's sister had gone: k Turn dies, in few

to dawn,
    Clean out of necessity, get there slowly.
thereupon, Through me in it sweat at
walk,
Have I heavy cold witty;

I had to pay dearly for that playing,ah, what
have I pain had:
I may not eat this, then that; k slept also
sometimes not by pain;
And I wish continuously know,
Or It hast done would are.
I didn't like reading, writing, Yes even in
mine prints not;
And to stay in bed for so long Gave me every
time a lot of sadness.
Father wanted to entertain me; Mother
sweet did, what they could;
But they had to stop immediately,k Used to
be it already tired honor I began.
I feared it would never work And when I
empty fed up,
Did I get very bad moods, while I no
patience more had.
I said in the end - that empty beingCan tog
never advantageous are.
I took a book; I went to do some reading;
And I felt fewer pain.
I also started writingAnd when I prints saw,
Could I on mine room to stay, Of
entertainment, Pine tree heal day.
Father once saw me start At An little
drawing,

Mother dear came in there, To at to see how
   it of me went.
   k Used to be, she didn't see, well at peace;
      I wasn't grumpy as before; k talked now
   and than at sometime mead;
      I didn't say *yes* or *no* . Like this worn out
   I gandsche to dawn,
      Clean, but not recovered, But that mope
   and that complain,
      Hasn't tormented me since. Father say, it
   can more to happen,
   That I not prosperous am;
But I will grieve the less, How I more over
   there On used to.
      Who can conform to God's will, (says he)
   with a still mind, Tastes in disease even
   pleasure;
God is always show and Good.
Farewell now, dear girls! Any in us house
   desires,
That puts an end to your journeys, If ye
   these letter received.

The swallows.

..... that is called first right on are entertainment at to live.

The swallows One narration

Kees would go to school for the first time,
But used to be the sidewalk pass resigned,
Or not shin, he used to be not well at
peace;
And stood, head held high, for a while in
astonishment. He saw the swallows Like
this to and again float,
And said, that's called living rightly to
one's pleasure first. A man That zig on
street found,
And Keesje understood ras, pulled it,
already smiling, what ter sides;
And said, well knowest thou not that they
must do this, They catch flies to feed their
young, That otherwise hungry had to
suffering.
Do you call this bad entertainment, no,
Keesje! that's wrong But know ye what
here out for you at learn is?
They may, through this merrily soaring,At
you An example to give,
How to do one's work with diligence and
joy; And that It ugly stands, if man it
forced do.

* * *

I walk Unpleasant school, said Kees: That
lesson is Certainly Good!

The Sun.

How big must God not orphans!

The Sun

When I see the sun shining, The one with
her sweet rays This earth cheerfully
cherishes;On that there spices to grow,
To feed cattle and man; That the light
makes us enjoy, To work happily, And
pleased at to live;
Than think I, of worship, How great must
God be!That Sun has he created!
And that out single love!

It corpse.

My dear children, do not be afraid, When
ye dead people sees;

It corpse

My dear children, do not be afraid, When
ye dead people sees;
   Would you tremble at corpses? Come
hither: this pale cold man, That to feel, to
see, nor to belong can,
Holds now not on at to live.

He thinks and works - yes more than you;
But of no body Like this if We.
The soul is away by the soil.
That God whom he has here feared, Is bee
it in are dead been;
And holds this corpse in value.

Already is the soul by it body off, Though
the corpse descends into the dark grave,
That must you not doing ice.
Believe it, good God Shall even this ugly
surplus
A lot of cleaner doing arise.

Ah, dear children! then don't say; What is
that die An sadness!
   May I but live forever! When you love
and serve God, Than performs the dead
you, if An friend,
In it forever blissful to live.

And when the last day comes, Than shall
It body, that over there lay,
Zig living weather show.
Then the Angels sail from below YOU
singing Unpleasant Pine tree Heaven to,
To forever over there at live.

My dear children, do not be alarmed,
When ye dead people sees;
   Would you tremble at corpses? Say
rather merry - this man, That here not to
see or hear can,
Allowed in Pine tree heaven to live.

It bird nests.

k Have now, said she, mine desire:

he bird's nestOne narration

Mietje once had, while walking, A concealed bird nests
In An thorn hedge found it.
I now have, Zeize, my desire:O How shall I me entertain,
With those sweet little animals! I'm going home to get some To this litters in at to put away.

Mietje walked and saw her mother, That she panting this told:

Dear Mietje, said the mother, Disturbing tog never bird's Nest!
Just think, how the ancient birds For that disturbance would mourn; would thou, Sissy sweet, not cry, If man you, of Pete and Jeez,
Transported against will; sis dear, have pity, Of That old dear birds!
Never seek your pleasure anyway In the sadness by An other.

No, said Sissy, dear mother!
No not that! but hear her cry; Ah she to have such hungry!

Don't think girl, said the mother, That

they just cry out of hunger. Ah she would
Certainly die,
If thou wilt feed them so long, Until they
couldn't scream anymore. But if you want
to have fun, And see how the old care To
them correct Like this a lot of at to give,
If the animals need Sets you bad in Silence
lower,
And you will soon notice, May they be
flies, mosquitoes, worms To catch and in it
litter to take.
o The good wise Creator Likes these birds
Parents, if given to you: These know
always better,
What the kids need Because they love
most. Yes they will never fail To care for
them tenderly; Therefore their God has
love Created for their young; And ye must
not pointer being,
Than the good and manner Creator.

Mietje listened to her mother; But often
went to see zagtken To the growing of the
boy, Without it litters ever at disturb.

flippy, the father, and the gardener.

Your father has Please good   pears:

flippy, the father, and the gardener

FLIP

Well, why do you prune the trees, Say loyal
  Pete?
Where those twigs would bear fruit, equal
  sees.

THE GARDENER

A tree that bears too muchloses are strength;
Nor would the fruit thus please,If ye expects.
  Your father has Please good pears:

THE FATHER

  it Is well said:
And the part of those who covet too much Is
  through bad.

The loneliness.

That entertainment has in It read, need
no loneliness at fear,

The loneliness

Don't think, dear playmates! That the time
me has to grieve,
    When I sat alone yesterday. That
entertainment has in It read,
Don't fear loneliness But is always well at
love.

Father says that, good people Often
Unpleasant That hours wish;
    often go to their room, In old and new
books Mode classes look up:
And that stands me miracle On.

I would like to be wise And I become also
Please praised,
    I say, as it comes to me: Should there be,
then, to know much, Many hour yet worn,
Welcome! welcome! loneliness!

Appendix
Collaboration between Jacob and Henry

HENDRIK
Thou knows you classes not, and hops however pleased.

JACOB
What hits It learn me?

HENDRIK
What hits It learn me? Thou may your Father fear.

JACOB
Serve can I well well-read.

HENDRIK
He said you recently yet, that ye An simpleton are.

JACOB
Whoa! Whoa! I have yet time.

HENDRIK
But if ye bigger are, than shall it you clear to bore.

JACOB

That can you few care.

HENDRIK

Very a lot of; I have you sweet, and fear there therefore for.

JACOB

Thou are An smart ass; hear!

HENDRIK

Now, it shall mine debt not are, gets ye by Father to succeed.

JACOB

Thou will That also not wear.

HENDRIK

And however see k not Please, that COOSJE to succeed gets.

JACOB

walk, silly Boy! silent.

HENDRIK

come, put your prick toll away, and get in time your books.

JACOB

I must there yet Unpleasant to search.

HENDRIK
Well hast you than; so not, than comes ge clear at leave.

JACOB
Yes, tomorrow! Best mate!

HENDRIK
Farewell than; it is mine time. I want to no bone muzzle being.

JACOB
I well, k have nothing at fear.

HENDRIK
Play than, so long it you lust: Thou are An silly son.

JACOB
What runs That prick toll beautiful!

* * *

Thou children, That this is reading, Wien praises ye well It most?

The snacking dogOne narration

A young man saw Pine tree canine That in the blessing his lords was standing Snap a taken chicken. In this way, he

cried, this moment is my most memorable opportunity; k Have your karma currently lengthy jealousy;
Presently I will appropriately applaud you. Yea, make you succeed, Until ye previously wailing sets down.

Rapidly he travels to his dad, And looked for, than above, than am a,
Until he was unable to relax. At the point when in the end he saw his Dad, When gotten down on he crying: 'Father! ok!
Will ye Lizet now not pay?
That canine you love so a lot, That take however everything what he finds.

That chicken that my Mom purchased, While she companions had mentioned,
To eat with us this evening, Lizet followed her to the steady; He had, the amount I yelled, it as of now
Eaten deep down. That appalling card absolutely faculties, That he your Dear puppies is.'

The Dad, who heard the enthusiasm, By which the kid until it came,

Also, until are bitterness had heard,

That PIETJE at times expands with lament, And presently out retribution or out envy
Zoo hurriedly until it used to be come,
Told him: 'Delicately, my PIETJE , delicately! Have ye your case well overthought?

Lizet has Surely awful finished, And k would it without uncertainty to beat,
Yet, I saw you walk so furiously, Zoo hot-tempered, that your dad fears,
Or on the other hand ye not furious are been;
Don't have any idea; I would rather not trust: Yet let me know if you're exhausted That occasionally your dad of it plays?'

Us PETE was quiet: - he became frightened, And it shin, he used to be are obligation cognizant;
You could see the response on his cheeks. 'However, Father!... indeed but...' he then, at that point, expressed out loud, 'Whatever had he of dish by doing?
He would much prefer get rabbits. On the off chance that I began what he did Than used to be mine discipline sure prepared.'

'Come,' said the Dad, 'tune in, Piet!
Presently salad I it without a doubt not;
It is envy that you come to denounce him;
It's jealousy, Pete! since this monster Me
at times is until diversion been.
Could you hence not bear him? Have I at
any point adored that creature?
Straightforwardly on the off chance that
you?. Fie! furious youngster!'

PIET looked humiliated, yet shed a tear.
Passes on talked are Father it So On:
"He who is furious consistently spreads
the word,
Also, remove bliss from their
hopelessness, Yet won't ever until their
advantage talk:
Indeed, on the off chance that he them
cherished sees, Gunt he their it light in the
eyes not.
Isn't that a delightful painting? Who has
straightforwardly? I, PETE ! or on the
other hand you?
Need ye yet longer furious being?'....
PIET was disheartened, delicately spilled
away; Men heard A craps yet are sobbing,
Furthermore, on it in LA FIT read.
It is said that never such an objection
Through PETE weather conditions

became   delivered.

Epilogue
Origin history

Toward the start of 1778 the Utrecht distributer Van Terveen distributed * an immaterial one group, named Proeve van Kleine Gedigten voor Kinder . It contained 24 sonnets, That to be sure typically not more space steamed up than one page octavo print. Outlines were absent, while the cover sheet was not creator's name expressed. Be that as it may, there was a short foreword, wherein the obscure writer are aim made sense of. He realize that he of It told, scholarly spoken, little popularity. Yet, he, being a dad of small kids himself, needed to them and to different youngsters between the ages of five and ten something valuable and simultaneously understandable at read to give as that in The Netherlands not prior used to be attempted and tried.

Could somebody promptly speculated to have Who That unknown youngsters' writer used to be? For each situation, the last option was absolutely mixed up in believing that he was managing such basic stanzas would assume little acknowledgment. Going against the norm, they are the main sonnets of his hand that stay in the memory of the Dutch public and that are name honey bee It extraordinary crowd living to have held.

Lang has the vulnerability about the initiation of the Proeve van Kleine Sonnets for Kids, as it turns out, didn't stand the test of time. Since still around the same time 1778 Van Terveen distributed a Spin-off with 22 sonnets in a similar style, again with no representation. This time, nonetheless, the author spread the word if mr. JOSH DOUGLAS ..

The Utrecht legal counselor Hieronijmus van Alphen was a decent one around then thirties. † As a man of letters he had made a few name in a restricted circle by a couple of heaps of illuminating verse and a couple of researcher compositions. Social and secretly anyway had he until up to this point not many karma

* The Koninklijke Bibliotheek The Hague holds under sign. 133 M 43 one out of 1943 from the chronicle Terveen obtained assortment by 244 nos. of 'Correspondence and Others pieces

concerning the Version by [.s] to work, predominantly by Little Sonnet For Youngsters '. She covers the period 1793-1872.

† Broad about it and are work: JOSH DOUGLAS 1973.

known. Attorney without business, was his young spouse on August 13, 1775 Johanna Maria van Goens passed on in labor. She had him as a single man abandoned with three young men: Jantje (immersed 7 February 1773), Daniël (sanctified through water 11 September 1774) and Hieronijmus (submersed 20 August 1775). That framed by the pre-declaration to the Proeve van Kleine Gedigten 'now just and most prominent delight'. For them as well, these youngsters' sonnets were first organization composed. Also, study and verse gave the fundamental interruption, by which are brother by marriage Rijklof Michael by Goens (A sibling by the dead

'Johnny') it Please aside was standing if guide in the cutting edge European writing.

How unreliable . himself about this time understood turns most plainly out his composed inquiries for character examination to Johann Kaspar Lavater in Zurich, That when for half Europe assuming specialist happened. In any case, the well known man answered in 1777 cool-dismissing; he previously had such a lot of correspondence to direct. After a year Van Alphen himself was a superstar: both as a result of his likewise in 1778 distributed Hypothesis of Expressive arts and Sciences (the primary Dutch Handbook on Current Style) * as by being 'Vaersjes voor Kinder', based on which Betje Wolff called it 'one of our most memorable Virtuoso and Best Writers' † referenced.

One republish of his two assortments of youngsters' sonnets has now showed up after the Others, with the goal that distributer By Terveen ten at long last of numbering halted to are stream rate for the opposition mysterious at to hold. It helped not many, on the grounds that before long flowed there are likewise a wide range of burglary prints. That could slip through the cracks since there was no copyright at this point existed.

More regrettable was Van Alphen's kindred townsman, the head master Pieter 't Hoen (1744-1828), it promptly imitated of An additionally secretly distributed New Preliminary Of Klijne Sonnets For Kids , written in 1778-1779 by Samuel de Waal and G. van cave Edge Jansz. showed up in Utrecht. The entire comprised of six 'bits' of altogether 126 sonnets. Two-faced enough did it grouse It in are review forestall or are child not longer had have the option to look out for It Through Van Alphen guaranteed Continuation of his Proeve , so he could do it without anyone's help kids' sonnets used to be beaten. Likewise this impersonation knew any amazing good fortune: It first piece experienced four, the second piece three and the third piece two. Well one proof that man assuming kids' artist in 1778 on A gold vein exhausted.

. is incidentatlly by That entire exchange no penny pointer become.

* See for this viewpoint Jacqueline the man 1998.

† E. cup, marry. A. Wolff, Taste about the childhood , Amsterdam's Hague 1779, p. 59.

He wild at no cost in the event that hack checked become and wonderful just in his job as a youngster's companion, witness the melodious words in the prelude to his subsequent group:

Tears stream from my eyes, Dear kids, on the off chance that you me asks to more verse.

However, achievement additionally invigorates the interest for more, with the goal that Van Alphen has proactively joined distribution by this quick subsequent group implied at must to apologize. It was, he guaranteed, not the slightest bit out of hesitance that his perusers would stand by so lengthy for a spin-off had should look. The matter used to be that verse himself not force let. He needed to as a writer basically holding on until he got once more into that state in which he are first group composed had.

Then, at that point, endured It spacious long term, until 1782, honor . of A Second Continuation of the Little Sonnets for Youngsters showed up. This third group counted twenty sonnets, by which It opening stanza 'At mine little perusers' min or more assuming that foreword served. Most importantly, they shouldn't feel that Van Alphen will fail to remember them used to be. The evidence was this, 'conceivably' his 'last pack'. For sure it turned out case.Ter shutting became in 1787 just yet the 66 sonnets out Taste , (First) and Second Spin-off as an assortment joined under the title Kleine Sonnets for Kids . Furthermore, they have been distributed as one booklet from that point onward. Distributer By Terveen had with that quite by It begin bill held by a ceaseless pagination of the three separate pieces. Additionally on the request by the 66 sonnets turned out to be rarely more altered.

After 1782, Van Alphen composed not any more youngsters' sonnets, not even before the kids out are second wedding, in 1781 Shut of Catherine Gertrude by Valkenburg. His situation in the public eye was because of his arrangement in July 1780 to Principal legal officer in Utrecht totally different. The political commotion of the Nationalist time later the religious undertakings pulled are consideration even more off by the writing. Wei are from his bequest in 1836 two additional kids' sonnets ('Cooperation among Jakob and Hendrik' and 'The nibbling canine'). come, That here assuming Informative supplement are printed.

It first Dutch children's book?

Writing has no right of patent, just like the case in the realm of applied sciences science and innovation is the situation. However Hieronijmus van Alphen introduced are Taste by Little Sonnet For Kids if A Dutch scoop. Legitimately or wrong? That simply relies upon what you mean by a kids' book accepts at to hear. The matter is on this point equivalent of the ask or Wolff and Covers History by

Miss Sarah Burger heart out 1782 our most memorable Dutch novel might be called. No, to the extent that there are additionally a lot of them for that year unique Dutch books have been distributed. Indeed, when you do that implies that Sara Burgerhart is toward the start of another sort in the Netherlands novel, that basically varies by what there before on that area at purchase used to be.

Back now Disagreeable .s Taste by Little Sonnet For Kids . Surely is that Van Alphen in both scholarly historiography and general assessment is viewed as the dad of the Dutch kids' book. * Obviously that is beyond the realm of possibilities imply that Dutch kids never read books before 1778. There are even great grounds to On at to take that in It eighteenth century The Netherlands, where the Huge A/B/C/or 'rooster book', the Maxims of Solomon and the little one drill were on the menu of each and every people school, relatively less uneducated people than in the other European nations. For the Protestant piece of individuals here used to be Book of scriptures perusing holy person obligation. Also, reading material for school use or for private home training have forever been there. Such showing materials changed after 1778 genuine not on fight.

What's more existed there in the eighteenth century likewise a wide range of recreation perusing for youthful and old without age distinction: by modest, of crude woodcuts embellished reprints by late middle age chapbooks if Reinaert , Ulenspiegel or The Four Heemschildren , yet more established tales by Aesop and Phaedrus, energizing travel reports about the seventeenth century captain Spotted cow, scriptural and profane picture books, puzzle-and assortments of stories until It most modest 'funny cartoon' of the penny print distributed in the city. † All that lay there in overflow, maybe not in the shop window by A respectable huge city book shop, yet than Anyway in the endless little ones shops Where individuals additionally their chronological registry or stationery* See for the accompanying: Pomes 1908; Dollar 1950; JOSH DOUGLAS 1990, 1992, 1995 and the Catalog of Dutch school and youngsters' books 1700-1800 by JOSH

DOUGLAS and Leontine JOSH DOUGLAS -
Smets, Zwolle 1997.
† See The Meyer 1962.

could purchase. Or probably there were
the endless colporteurs who honor the
colder time of year came, they ventured
to every part of the field to their well
known houses and homesteads to wear
out perusing. What's more, that sluggish
inclination of frequently republished for a
really long time famous perusing Stayed
temporary likewise after 1778 yet Quiet
wave on.

Notwithstanding, there is one central
contrast between those conventional ones
recreation perusing, Where little and
enormous Terrible grasps, and the Taste
by which . in 1778 for the day came and
on ground of which he legitimately the
Maker by the advanced Dutch youngsters'
book might be called. That distinction was
not in it whether admonishing. That a
book, regardless of how engaging, is
dependably valuable and Instructive
needed to are utilized to be for everybody
A split up case. It new ones hides in here
that . himself if first explicitly until small
kids pointed of An understandable to

them and never before in the Netherlands in such an alluring way introduced educational task.

What did this new ideal of training seem to be and what way did Van Alphen take on that track come?

The new ones pedagogy

In the event that dad by three little men became mr. JOSH DOUGLAS in the years seventy naturally looked of It issue by their childhood. What's more, the enlightened reasoning . used to be there the man not Upsetting to, if individuals by stand when yet frequently did, to pass on such a profound errand to a lead representative. He liked to arrange himself individual in the ongoing writing, in which the new ones bits of knowledge about schooling were engendered.

The subject of how best to serve one's own or others' youngsters to raise appears from the years sixty lightning quick by A moderately plainly obvious matter until A most noteworthy hazardous matter at are developed. Instructional method (It word just as of now is than new!) turned out to be unexpectedly something Where each enlightened regular citizen to stress over, in light of the fact that it is to bring about some benefit for both the individual and the country by depended. Who, on the off chance that the Edification ideologues, unshakable had confidence in the manufacturability of a general public with sensible and thusly normally highminded residents had after the very Best an open door by to prevail of the childhood by the young.

Where came That enlightened instructional method Like this out of nowhere from? Which creators to have her arranged? Furthermore, what outcomes has that had for the Dutch youngsters' book? Obviously there is compelling reason need to uncertainty the response for a really long time: generally Locke, Rousseau and Basedow (with in a more far off point of view Comenius) on the off chance that the envoys by this new ones teaching method, That It youngster in are singularity finds and That himself likewise earnestly appears in A new sort kids' book.

The Brit John Locke owes his spearheading job to a generally in 1693 distributed composition: A few considerations concerning Schooling . * It work became in 1753 through the interpretation of Pieter Adriaen Verwer again to the consideration from the Dutch public. Locke put extraordinary accentuation on the playing learning in opportunity, at the end of the day: on the learning joy that a youngster ought to have the option to do to have. A reverberation of this sounds yet Through in .s line of refrain 'Mine to play is learning, my gaining is playing' from 'Advancing cheerfully'. That gaining existed for the dull Locke mostly from helpful information obtaining. To music or verse he didn't squander many words. As kids' perusing, he particularly suggested the tales by Aesop On, best of pictures.

While in this manner Lockes composition in the years sixty It banter about the childhood weather conditions enacted, made Jean Jacques Rousseau in a ton of more extensive circle disturbance of his Émile, ou de l'Education (1762). † In convincing style here turned into the ideal training depicted and showed to the instance of the youthful Émile, who, far by the acculturated (= ruined) world, A regular childhood got.

Fundamental example by this clique book for the New ones Man used to be the adage: leave betijen, force nothing off. The youngster will normally get familiar with the unsaid truth through experimentation follow the case of his instructor. There is additionally no impulse in educating furious. It is particularly off-base to fill kids with real information, of which they It utility and the extension yet not see. Everything comes on understanding and in this manner keep away from to irritate a youngster with strict conventions. That last one was Normally as a trade-off for It sore leg kicked by every single christian teacher.

By state, Rousseaus became Émile following showing up on 11 July Consumed transparently in Paris in 1762. In any case, over the long haul, the impact of his educational thoughts likewise in The Netherlands reasonable been, she It frequently in a roundabout way through the German philanthropies. ‡ Their foreman used to be Johann Bernard Basedow, the pioneer in 1774 by It Philanthropinum at Dessau, A model school Where underneath It careful focus of all Europe the illuminated thoughts regarding training with German Gründlichkeit were tried interestingly. Those standards were: support to self-inspiration;

* See additionally Samuel F. pickering, John Locke and Kids' books in Eighteenth

Century Britain , Knoxville (Ten.) 1981.

† See Walter Gobbers, Jean Jacques Rousseau in Holland. An exploration Upsetting the impact by the man and It work (approx. 1760-ca. 1810) , Ghent 1963; unique part IV: welcome by 'Emile'.

‡ See AWM duijx, The philanthropies. List of sources by in The Netherlands present books by JB Basedow, JH camp and BC G. Salzman , To lead 1985.

actual solidifying; visual schooling, outfitted towards helpful citizenship; moral training in an overall Christian sense through lecturing portrayals; kid cordial estimate as per A complex framework by to rebuff and rewards. One composed by Basedow himself filled in as a 'course book' Elementarwerk (1774), luxuriously represented with many copper etchings by the well known Daniel Chodowiecki.

The Philanthropinum at Dessau was essentially a pricey organization, just reasonable for youngsters out the first class. In any case, what primarily surprising drag used to be It around there showed display: the penetrating techniques, the public tests of a great deal of horns and to call and the before long breaking out clashes between the dictator Basedow and are staff. In the Netherlands, the response to this was accordingly with blended sentiments humanitarian analysis. Just in Amsterdam started sure Alexandre Des-Londes in 1781 likewise A such 'Maison d'Education' for 24 students as per Basedow's framework. * based on the plates from his Elementarwerk examples would be given in French and Dutch language, geology, regular history, history, work out, to compose and to draw, while A military every day tumbling training came to give. The school day endured by s mornings eight to nine PM, with ƒ 65 for outer understudies and ƒ 65 for interior understudies even needed to pay ƒ105 per quarter. In any case, regular enough know we this Basedowse school at Amsterdam single out An opportunity safeguarded roundabout and know we nothing about the viable execution. Basedows Rudimentary work additionally tracked down just a single supporter in the Netherlands: the German teacher JD Hahn Utrecht. Interpreted is It here never. More effective were the compositions of two different altruists: Joachim Heinrich Campe, the main kids' book writer from this circle, who after Basedows constrained takeoff the line by It Dessauer Philanthropinum dominated, and Christian Gotthilf Salzmann, who in 1783 at Schnepfenthal own instructive establishment. Their ethical stories and reflections are likewise broadly perused, deciphered and altered in the Netherlands. Their impact on it Dutch kids' book appears to be impressive, in spite of the fact that we actually escape us of that impact all nuances. †

* See IH by Eeghen, 'A cutting edge Basedowse school in Amsterdam', in: month to month magazine
Amstelodamum , jrg. 48 (1961), p. 129-132.
† See Erfahrung schrieb's und reicht's der Jugend. Joachim Heinrich Campe as Kinder-und Jugendschriftteller . Ausstellungskatalog Staatsbibliothek Berlin, 1996; and Visionare Lebensklugheit. Joachim Heinrich Campe in seiner Zeit (1746-1816) , Wiesbaden 1996 (Ausstellungskatalog Herzog August library Wolfenbuttel).
With all that justifiable consideration for different new instructive motivations

from an external perspective, nonetheless, we ought not be ignorant concerning two a lot more seasoned locals nurturing customs: a Christian humanist, where Felines, Van Effen and others eighteenth-century observers, whom the youngster sees as a plant that can be framed with delicate power. What's more, a severe Improved, who the full accentuation lays on the principled corruption by each man and the trepidation des Respectable men considers as the chief method for discipline, * as occurs in De Geestelycke Queeckerye by the Youthful Plants des Noble men [...] Or to parcel by the Christelycke Training of Youngsters (1740) by the Middelburg head master Joannes The Swaf. In the two methodologies, notwithstanding, the consideration and furthermore the adoration represented it youngster focused, so the frequently introduced portrayal of a preceding existing indifferent parent-kid relationship totally needs remedy. † Likewise the picture of the seventeenth or eighteenth century head master as a domineering jerk with free hands and ever parched throat ‡ appears to be not in excess of A cartoon That Through the enlightened educators honey bee their development hostile yet as of now at Please became utilized.

Like this turns out the world by It youngsters' book as well as It more extensive landscape by instructive training is a nation of two streams, where old and new coincide to walk. By the two has . on sovereign way utilized. Are Little Sonnet For Youngsters are now and again suggestive with regards to content or in their utilization of pictures Locke, Rousseau and the German philanthropies, than climate On the old felines, as in the notes here for every individual sonnet are shown. Yet, farther than A shallow parallelism go That understanding never.

* See B. Kruithof, 'Instructive Counsel from Felines to Beets, Coherence and Assortment', in: Schooling and Childhood 1983, p. 169-178; LF Groenendijk, The Further Reconstruction of It family. The vision by Peter White curd on the christian housekeeping , Dordrecht 1984.

† About the spot of, the consideration for and the vision of the youngster in the seventeenth and eighteenth hundred

years, a whole library has now been filled. It's just plain obvious, among others: Linda Pollock, Neglected Children. Parent-Youngster Relations from 1500 to 1900 , Cambridge 1983; Keith thomas, 'Kids in Early Present day britain', in: Gillian Avery and Juliet Briggs (ed.), Children and their books. A Festival of Crafted by Iona and Peter Opie , Oxford 1990, p. 45-77; JOSH DOUGLAS , 'The Little Republic; the family in Dutch writing of the eighteenth 100 years', in: Documentatieblad Werkgroep Eighteenth Hundred years , jrg. 24 (1992), p. 87-105; Sally Kevill Davies, The previous Children. The collectibles and history or youngster care , Woodbridge 1994; Rudolf Dekker, Out of the shadow into the incredible light. Youngsters in self image reports of the Brilliant Hundred years until the Sentiment , Amsterdam 1995.

‡ [CF van Veen] in: Kids read/youngsters read , show list no. 195 of Metropolitan Exhibition hall Amsterdam, 1958, p. 6.

Two German predecessors: Weisse and Burmann

Van Alphen is never secretive about two more direct sources of inspiration done. In It preview until are *Taste* calls he if such Weisses *song fur Kinder* [Leipzig 1767/1769] and the *Kleine Lieder für kleine Mädchen und Jünglinge* [Berlin 1777] by Gottlob William Burmann.

The philanthropist Christian Felix Weisse (1726-1804) was one of the philanthropists in Germany first writers That their pen absolutely ten employ suggested by the youth. * He acquired great popularity with his weekly magazine *Der Kinderfreund* (1776-1782), which is also published in the Dutch became edited, while are *Neues ABC Book* (1772) our compatriot Jan Henry Swildens inspired until are *patriotic AB Book for the Dutch Youth* (1781). No wonder that Van Alphen with such authority on pedagogical area happy to correspond. †

Because what Mr. Hieronijmus in 1778 for The Netherlands of are first bundle children's poems wild to test, that had Weisse in 1767-1769 already reached for Germany with his *Lieder für Kinder* .

Weisse's bundle must also have addressed Van Alphen in this way, because the German poet had also recently become a father for the first time and these songs for made his own children. In addition, he found the whole in Weisse's songs virtues of the Christian Enlightenment in a way that appeals to children manner worded.

. owned by Weisse are *Little lyrical Poem* (Leipzig 1772), in which all fifty-four 'Lieder für Kinder' were also recorded. Van edited from this Alphen seven poems: 'Der Horsam' ('It dogs'), 'Der Krausel' ('The floating top), 'That Freundschaft' ('The true friendship'), 'Der Winter' ("Winter Song"), 'That Mucke' ('The insolence'), 'Auf das Bildniß einer geliebten Mutter' ('Claartje at the painting by hers deceased mother') and 'Das Bird's Nest' ('It birds' nests').

The now whole forget Gottlob William Burmann (1737–1805) [‡] made any name of fables in the style by Gellert. Are children's poems goods, just if That by Weisse, provided by yourself manufactured melodies. But he missed service visual assets, so that even bee agreement by theme the effect whole otherwise is becoming. In instead of making his little heroes speak themselves as a child, he always puts them in all sorts long-winded, abstract contemplative

* See about Weisse and are *song fur children* : Brüggemann 1982, k. 86-93 and 1250.

† This correspondence between . and Weisse seems unfortunately lost at are gone.

‡ See about GW Burmann and are children's songs: Brüggemann 1982, k. 1298-1299.

yellowing in the mouth. Exemplary is Burmann only been Through the introduction by the new patriotic sentiment in children's poetry. Van edited from his collection Alphen four poems: 'Allgemeines bet' ('The true wealth'), 'Der Mirror' ('The mirror'), 'Vaterlandsliebe' ('The love until It Native country') and 'Thank you one Knaben beym Witter' ('It storm').

If you put those eleven example poems side by side like this, Van Alphens shines tributary On Weisse and Burmann not slight. But he spoke the truth, when he stated that she it well many times on Pine tree away assisted' had, but that he there actually no out 'translated, or taken over' had. Accurate comparisonleave soon to see how big the differences are, whereby . It if poet usually wins against Weisse and certainly against the solemn Burmann. [*]

Still understand one why Van Alphen's children's poems in neighboring Germany are never any gained popularity. They looked just a little too much like what was already there for that amply in original existed.

Literary aspects: It quality mark by the relief

Van Alphen's youngsters' sonnets vary in structure and content from all that what was written in the Netherlands around then. Unique is as a matter of some importance the pregnant structure: even more striking since Dutch writers, particularly on the off chance that they intended to establish, when scarcely by to hold up knew. Refrains by ten, fifteen verses with many guidelines were no exemption. The language is likewise the very Normally that the short text Through single read currently in It memory printed became.

Inside that restricted extension, there is an astounding assortment in line length, refrain structure, rhyme conspire, musical overshadowing, themes and sort structures. One tracks down lovely stories there (frequently awesome, basically the most well known sonnets, for example, 'The plum tree' and 'The messed up glass'), exchanges, a rhyming letter ('Carel to his sister Caatje'), the connected one case ('Welcome good tidings from Claartje for her younger sibling'), verses ('The Singing Willem') lastly that enormous gathering that the representative application by A preceding portrayed creature or item related is On It symbol (for instance 'It canines' or 'The bird on the stool').

* For the relationship see: Pomes 1908, p. 244-259, and van Eck Jr. 1908, p. 225-238, with inverse end. As per Pomes was standing . writer honey bee Weisse than honey bee Burman, which By Eck battles. The fundamental measure is the iamb or trochee, yet in three cases we track down

an entire land and water proficient stanza. Exceptional is 'The singing Willem', where (after a story presentation in ordinary versifying measure) Willem are honorable morning tune in tribute structure. Similarly amazing is that Van Alphen is even in his youngsters' sonnets didn't avoid exploring different avenues regarding rhymeless verse. A six sonnets, under which the known individual ' Portrayal by Dorisje', needed to It proof to convey that man beneath specific circumstances 'the country around there On simple would become acclimated to'. *

Notwithstanding this variety in shape, the entire actually establishes an extremely homogeneous one connection because of the ethos of the Illumination that penetrates everything. The Little Sonnets for Youngsters are additionally Similar to this tricky straightforward that man barely more has an eye on what their most unique quality is: Van Alphens remarkable resources for in extremely pregnant language and in It briefest potential particulars A totally norms design, that by the delicate Alleviation, height at to give.

The youngsters' reality evoked here is

over totally portrayed by a feeling of happiness, of 'lively' if watchword. A productive, cautious youngster has after all nothing to fear: not from father who is his 'closest companion'; not of God who called us 'to made joy', and surely not of the boogeyman. Demise additionally has nothing frightful and the nature is dependably Great, in any event, when It tempest. All rode So until merriment, appreciation and fulfillment: attributes Where later sexual orientations have left the stamp of homegrown revoltingness on them, yet those for the edified regular citizen out the eighteenth century the most noteworthy structure by karma made up. Honey bee merriment one should positively not consider any type of loud diversion, but rather to that inward and consistent happiness that comes from science: everything strolls in this world as it is planned by a savvy God as long as I have my obligation do.

For a youngster from the wealthy working class climate to which Van Alphen himself had a place the last option basically implied: learning his illustrations. Despite the fact that there is no lawful one yet obligatory training existed and such youngsters for the most part just confidential home instruction the need forintellectual schooling was however perfect as it seems to be today . As per the worth scale by the Alleviation was standing information straightforwardly of ethicalness. Who inept Stayed botched likewise the opportunity of being a full person. Moreover, great review execution is the premise lay for material abundance. Anyway stresses . in are kids' sonnets no place this social viewpoint. Learning joy starts things out. Learning must, every day; except to learn is likewise pleasant ('It bright learn'). Also, nothing more fun than A read* JOSH DOUGLAS from Alphen, Stomach related Compositions , Utrecht 1782, p. CXIX .

book of decent pictures, for what It conventional toys (band and cost) Please is shoved aside. That decision is given additional alleviation, on the grounds that fairly notwithstanding garments and food likewise the toys were considered as a part of the things that 'Innocent satisfaction's decide. Like this guarantees Little Claar in her 'Welcome hello' her little younger sibling that mother will likewise purchase toys for her, when she can sit on her lap. Is toys than in some cases something mediocre just in the extremely earliest stage however that ought to be traded for a course reading as quickly as time permits? Claire and Keetje talk about that It reclaiming word: 'In some cases to play, some of the time read,/Dat will well It Best being'.

The encounters and impressions of the youngsters from Van Alphen's Kleine gedigten remain generally limited to their own homegrown circle of father, mother, family of their close friends. It family relationship stands focal, by which the adoration connection between the guardians vehemently is becoming confirmed. Such love needs no costly gifts: 'Father gave the best peach/recently to mother with a 'kiss'. Further family members (grandparents, uncles, aunties, cousins) waste time ter talk, neither if neighbors or companions by the family. A couple of time seems A grounds-keeper, An Others obliging or A coincidental bystander on It theater to honey bee fathers nonattendance if guide on at steps. Exceptional is the spot of high standing That . awards On the old cook

Saartje. Are ancestor Weisse had Upsetting own say at this point trusted of are 'moral' kids' sonnets An end at to make On 'the boring melodies by pastry specialist and babysitter'. * For kids' fantasies merchandise the most Illumination teachers certain hypersensitive, Betty Wolff not excepted. . then again portrays of clearly delight A kids' visit honey bee Sarah, 'Our old great cook,/Who can tell fantasies', 101 inquiries addresses and the youngsters on chocolatemilk treats.

More dangerous is turning into the intercourse of individuals That not until the own circle have a place. Cheerful turns out the city gatekeeper of are ratchet per balance A defender by hearth and family, while the cloth jew who thumps at the entryway may likewise be there unnerving looking however certainly not malevolent. appears to be more fierce the gathering in the road in the colder time of year cold with a flimsy hobo, 'who requests a dime supplicate'. That is becoming without a second thought datum, only if in the 'Winter Melody' occurs Yet it just builds up the sensation of appreciation for one's own prosperity and brings It trust in the stock organization no second On It falter.

Why additionally, when in 'It found it melodies' An unfortunate damn are fulfillment sings out and yourself makes sense of not of A rich man at need trade:

* 'kick the bucket abgeschmackten Lieder der Amme und Kinderwärterin' (Christian Felix Weissens Selbstbiography , 1806, p. 129).

The yearning I only occasionally miss, Do me a ton of more enthusiastic eat,

Then or I at a lord's table Used to be day On day situated.

Inverse this cultural traditionalism, that a couple of years after the fact additionally in The Netherlands extremist reformers like Gerrit Paape will prompt social dissent thoughts and sentiments that vouch for an illuminated brain. That new sit it above all else in the nonappearance by every strict doctrinalism. despite the fact that himself a proclaiming Christian, Van Alphen deliberately has generally doctrinal issues of unique sin, reclamation, heck, and paradise out of thought left. Taking everything into account, they just have a place in a later period of schooling to come to arrange.

All things considered, God becomes innocent understanding only in the event that A caring Dad recommended. Like this could It happens that Jantje and his companions in all actuality do get examples in perusing, composing, geology ('The great desire') and harpsichord playing ('Mietje bij het harpsichord'), however that they go to chapel, pastor or catechist saved stays.

They are by all accounts not the only side effects of an edified teaching method. We identify in .s kids' sonnets 'The affection until It Local country' additionally as of now It new ones enthusiastic feeling, which, it just so happens, is still liberated from party political understanding here from the 1980s, when Loyalists and Orangists faced each other at to stand. In that new ones enthusiastic inclination shows himself A soul by urban sense That as of now honey bee It small kid should become developed. It is A subject that Through Jan Hendrik Swildens in his Vaderlandsch Stomach muscle Book for the Dutch Youth (1781) model will become worked out. *

Be that as it may, who based on the above

Van Alphens youngsters' sonnets to the Edification writing works out, has yet the misleading statement said. It enlightened think knows after all in the eighteenth century a few changes Horrendous time, nature, strict shading and degree. Like this contrasts the French Help of its profligate inclination emphatically from the by and large Christian Edification in Germany and The Netherlands, while the mid eighteenth century Alleviation, of which Justus by plain of are Dutch Observer (1731-1735) A significant delegate used to be, considerably more accentuation on scholarly thinking than the delicate Illumination out the years seventy.
* See JOSH DOUGLAS , 'Dutch ABC books out the eighteenth hundred years; custom and development', in: Jaap Terlinden ea, A will be a Monkey. Expositions on ABC Books of the Fifteenth 100 years until present , Amsterdam 1995, p. 55-72.

How are the kids' sonnets by Hieronijmus van Alphen doing in this regard? The response can't be totally unequivocal. In certain spots we track down still the pure realism of contemplated prudence, as in

'De enterprising nature':
Could I invest my energy At thousand trivialities?
k Have around there no advantage by.
In a similar line is likewise the level-headed dismissal by all notion (in 'Klaasje and Pietje') by which the one little excellence the Others endeavors off at resources:
Pietje, if you would rather not be great, Then, at that point, the person of color shows up. Klaasje, that is clearly false! Allow him to come in the event that he would be able. Who has confidence in such a man, Is by are mind ransacked.
Notwithstanding,

Reception and valuation

Hieronijmus van Alphen has also manifested himself as a poet writer of literary-theoretical writings and as a Christian philosopher. Here, however go It single to the reactions on are children's poems, whereby That Others aspects hardly play a role. That simplifies things. But there remains a difficulty bypass problem: the children, for Who this texts However destined goods, come yourself of their judgement nowhere straight away in image.

Usually measure man It good luck by An literary work first of all off On It number reprints or translations and On the with that corresponding circulation figures. Unfortunately possess we on that point not about precise facts if consequence by It smoke screen laid by publisher Van Terveen. We only know for sure that the *Kleine Gedigten voor Kinder* up to around 1850 arranged in various versions reprinted are, while she short after to appear also already on music put became. After that, interest dropped sharply, even to such an extent that one started in 1871 jubilee edition (*Party gift for the Dutch youth*) it no further then released two episodes. Until publications by Pomes and Van Eck in 1908 the 'old-fashioned' children's poems by Van Alphen again under the attention, after which they, as it were, face a new life went: as a near-genuine, photographic reprint for non-pedagogical buyers lesson but An attractive gift booklet of nostalgic value searched.

How did Van Alphen's contemporaries and those immediately following generation of readers, *Small Poems for Children are* appreciated and why sudden 'nod' in the interest halfway through the previous century? [*]

The first to whom Van Alphen in 1777 presented his then unprinted *Proeve van Small Poem For Children* submitted used to be are brother in law Rijklof Michael by Goens. This found all poems Unpleasant form and contents for It goal suitable but had the collection Please yet extensive seen of 'any stories'. If before that two Others poems deleted had to become, than maybe 'The true friendship' and Alexis. The latter seemed to him too 'prosaic or abstract', while for the former the objection was that children do not have much idea of 'cuddling' or being 'cuddly' 'in Pine tree sentence in which We it conceive'. JOSH DOUGLAS had to but at sometime the trial on the sumtake with his son Jantje. [†] From the fact that Van Alphen criticized the two poems Ordinary has to leave to stand, to be allowed to we maybe to distract that at least An child to this are approval datum has.

In An later letter by 21-23 June 1800 pale By Goens yet for a bit enthusiastic ifa quarter of a century earlier: 'Die *Kinderlieder* sind wahre Meisterstücke, in ihre Art: so gut, if das best [...] was man in some Sprache hat.' [‡] Only now he came with An curious content-related argument Why .s children's poems even would still be preferable to that of Weisse, namely 'wegen den Christian Sinn, der in Pine tree Ihrigen herrscht'. This view testifies however more of the religious Réveil, contrary to the spirit of the Enlightenment, through which By Goens when inspired became, than that she straight did On .s *Small Poem For Children* , which precisely because of their lack of dogmatic lines some orthodox reviewers had raised objections. Clarisse for example, confessed that (with all due respect to Van Alphen) his line 'En tot happiness created' from 'The childlike happiness' was difficult for him to reconcile with the Calvinist predestination.[**]

* Such incidental criticism from the Orthodox Christian side, meanwhile, did not affect the least prejudice On .s fame if children's poet. And when imitation ItBest proof is for good luck, than can man say that .s children's poems for decades the show to have put in subject See also The Freeze 1981.

† Letter from RM van Goens to Hieronijmus van Alphen, undated [1777], K . B . 130 D 14.Compare J. Wille, *The man of letters RM van Goens and his circle* . Second Part, edited by P.by der Vliet. Amsterdam 1993, p. 246.

‡ See JOSH DOUGLAS , 'Letters by Rijklof Michael by Goens On JOSH DOUGLAS .', in: *Documentation sheet Working Group Eighteenth Century* XX /2 (1988), p. 175-176.

** Clarisse 1831-1832, p. 120.

choice and form. So much so that everything that was Dutch in those years children's poetry appeared a more or less faint echo of Van Alphen layman. Sometimes became that also Through later children's poets if Peter it grouse, Henry belt cutter, Dirk Underwater and JFL Muller openly recognized. [*]

In the mid-nineteenth century, however, Van Alphens gained a reputation as children's poet An formidable snap Through the accusation by unchildishness. Once
PA de Génestet in his verse story 'De Sint-Nikolaaseven' from 1849 is already a vicious blow to Hieronijmus, [†] came the same author in 1857 before the same hearing again on the matter. Its like rehabilitation intended lecture *On children's poetry* [‡] however, bore more of the character of one worked out prop, pass On It end what tempered Through An whiff sympathy for Van Alphen's good intentions. Geneset's objections are well known, because repeated a hundred times: it is a good Hendriken morale that

Van Alphen are hearing imprint, for a bit false if unhealthy. In place by child of the children at are, stilt . himself above are youthful audience.

That last is Certainly Where, as An anonymous critic already in 1798 had established. ** But equally true is that the 'firm boys, tough guys' mentality from which The Génestet who allegedly attacks pedantic goodness, in an equally time-bound ideal. This time not from the Enlightenment but from the Dutch Romance.

The Geneset appealed himself bee are attack on It according to it so much more lifelikefashion model by the Dutch boy that Hildebrand in are *Camera obscure* would to have outlined. But Beets yourself took It now for . on: what currently stiff seemed, used to be once, in the eighteenth century, fresh and original; they had to discuss it standing children's poems judge in It light by their own time.

How Where that also if are, It effect by The Gene sets criticism used to be

* See for these followers Wirth 1925, chapter III : 'In Van Alpha's footprint'.
† PA the geneset, 'Sint Nicholas Eve. An Amsterdam tale', stanza LXVII of

corresponding note; pass published in the reprint by are *First Poems* (1860).

‡ The Geneset 1858.

** 'Many, That by the upbringing knowledge mean at to have, and even books about that to write, show that they understand nothing of it. They speak, and reason, with the children, op a tone as if they had the same understandings and knowledge as they themselves have. [...] She know zig not in the place der children at set, and until theirs childish concepts lower at descend. By over there the little pedants, in the children's books at grouse, ., Perponcher and others.' (*Table of Morals, Education, Learning, Taste, and Enlightenment, in the former province of Holland, at the end of the eighteenth century. A contribution to the reform, of education and schooling, in the Batavian Republic* . By a' Cosmopolitan, Amsterdam 1798, p. 58-59).

that from now on Van Alphen's *Small Gedigten for Children* should be viewed with different eyes went to look at. She goods, to Like this at say, by the one day on the Others old-fashioned become. And It would more than An half century to last honor their prestige until new ones height would to rise, she It now (in scientific circle) if pedagogical-historical monument, or (with the general public) as a nostalgic reminder of a far past. A text That that reaches allowed pass straight classic to be named.

Mode by Edition

Compositions of Van Alphen's kids' sonnets are not known, and none duplicates with both text and plates in the earliest print unhesitatingly can be assigned. What one finds in early deliveries is generally obvious structures of various releases of Proeve, Vervolg and Tweede Vervolg of incidentatlly minute text-or accentuation contrasts. Just the sharpness by the inscriptions can change impressively, even inside one duplicate. Also, are honey bee such composite duplicates the different cover sheets normally remove and to supplant Through A general title.

Just since the approved aggregate release of 1787 does a specific normalization on, however this Occupied in duodecimo design stands currently An end off by the true 'Van Alphen with the lines'. This is, obviously, significantly more evident degree for the '. of the caps' out 1821, That solely interest esteem has.

The to this past text version is, what the Taste Re, in view of It duplicate by the main print out the Illustrious Library (sign. 1090 E 109) and for Spin-off and Second Continuation on duplicates of the principal release in my control of the most seasoned known individual (maybe first) print by the plates. To bigger security all texts are precise contrasted with other early duplicates, where the new bibliographical articles by LG Saalmink are significant method for control blanching.

For the two youngsters' sonnets distributed after death by Clarisse is here additionally the first packaged Occupied out 1836 followed. *

Our text version is entire strategic of protection by the first spelling and accentuation. That implies that likewise linked verbal

Clarisse, 'On Hieronijmus van Alphen, as writer and youngsters' artist. two readings, Rotterdam 1836.

are imitated precisely as they were initially printed. Improved are a couple of clear printing mistakes, which than in the explanation is becoming notice.

A text with such a long printing history has normally evolved throughout the years go through innumerable expected and accidental changes after some time:

changes of spelling, accentuation, utilization of words and once in a while likewise by contents. Since she anyway no of all have been applied by the writer himself and generally date from a lot later times, to have we she here on a couple of special case after external thought left. That special case Re the gatherer's version 1787, Where . probably yet well has supported. To the extent that that contrasted with the three before individual seemed packs until significant variations has driven, is additionally that in our explanation showed.

Weird as it might sound: Van Alphen's kids' sonnets are, notwithstanding them fixed place in the group by the Dutch writing never prior in clarified structure showed up. Their clear effortlessness made obviously for some every clarification superfluous. In the mean time is That plainly obvious coherence currently lengthy become a fiction. One might express that with such a basic figure of speech the sliding of the word significance and in this way the psychological distance among text and peruser It most clear noticeable is becoming. That now next A '. of the join's and A '. of the caps' for It first likewise A '. of nuts' sees the light, is thusly an important work to cover as wide as conceivable readership to connect that distance. Simultaneously, nonetheless, it marks perusing version It social interest by our eighteenth century youngsters' writing, for what mr.

JOSH DOUGLAS in 1778 the away has beaten.

Albeit this text release was practically prepared for press in 1995, it has to a wide range of reasons yet long term endured honor she likewise to be sure printed could turn into. This delay enjoyed the extra benefit that few late distributions around eighteenth-century kids' writing, all the more explicitly about youngsters' sonnets by JOSH DOUGLAS ., yet in epilog and comment consolidated could turn into.

Satisfy expresses gratitude toward I prof. dr. EK Grootes for are staff honey bee It planning by this Release and for are persistence of mine eagerness.

THE END

Description

"Small Poems For Children" is a magnificent assortment of verse intended to catch the minds of youthful perusers. From capricious stories of talking creatures to genuine reflections on kinship and family, this book offers a different scope of subjects and styles to engage a wide crowd of kids.

Whether you're perusing with your youngster before bed or searching for a great method for bringing verse into the study hall, "Small Poems For Children" is the ideal expansion to any youngsters' shelf. With its beguiling outlines and essential stanzas, this book makes certain to turn into a loved #1 long into the future.